**Edition Schott**

**Alvin Singleton**
b.1940

# In My Own Skin

for Piano

edited by Laura Gordy

**ED 30101**

www.schott-music.com

Mainz · London · Madrid · New York · Paris · Prague · Tokyo · Toronto
© 2013 SCHOTT MUSIC CORPORATION, New York · Printed in USA

# Foreword

The title of this one-movement highly-pianistic creation lets us know clearly where the composer is comfortable. But within that skin in this work are two competing sonic worlds. Beginning chorally in big harmonies, that mood is soon interrupted by loud running 16th note octaves.

Slow, strong, and measured then seems to face off against young, strong, and impetuous throughout the piece. Or perhaps consider it a dialogue between two strong players; one the Emersonian voice of quiet, time-seasoned reason and the other wild and quicksilver, both in tempo and in rhythmic variety. The drama of *In My Own Skin* lies within these disjunct phrases, as each seems to argue as to what the whole piece should be about. Jazz and classical implications also keep things interesting. Some might hear those opening chords not so much as a classical chorale as like jazz big-band brass and winds, the running 16ths as something out of Lenny Tristano or Thelonious Monk. Of course Singleton fans know that it is about both, sonic and cultural worlds which live in his skin in comfortable equality. At midpoint in the piece the composer inserts a sly almost-Caribbean tune that seems to try to quiet the controversy down a bit. But soon we are back at it, and as the work closes the voice of placid reason has the last word.

Carman Moore
2012

First Performance:

November 17, 2011
Roulette
Brooklyn, New York
Teresa McCollough, piano

*This piece was made possible by a grant from the Fromm Music Foundation*

*for Teresa McCollough*

# In My Own Skin

Alvin Singleton

ED 30101

November 4, 2010
MacDowell Colony

Duration: 10 minutes